never make a sound

a memoir

never make a sound

a memoir

*Dear Christine
Happy reading!*

fanen chiahemen

The Awakened Press

The Awakened Press
www.theawakenedpress.com

Cover and Interior Design by David Moratto

This book is a work of creative nonfiction and is a memoir.
It honestly reflects the author's true remembrance of real
experiences. The events, people, locales and conversations brought
to light are presented as accurately as possible in accordance with
the author's recollections. This book is of a self-help nature and
was created for the purpose of healing and growth. Although great
care has been taken to ensure that all characters and situations
are presented in a compassionate and respectable manner, others'
memories may be different than the author's own. The words are
based on truthful situations from the author's memory and are
her words alone, and the reader should not consider this book
anything other than a work of literature.

First edition.

ISBN 978-1-989134-15-3

contents

prologue

christmas time
holiday time
last good time
 ivory sands
  emerald seas
   shining slides
    blinding smiles
                    (eclipsing
      grinding poverty)
     barbeque lobster
    father christmas
                    we smile in those photos
          two little girls in oversized dresses, magenta,
      pinstriped charcoal
          bows on bows
          like wrapping paper
          too big dresses on too skinny girls
          I'm smiling arms out ready for the world
          new teddy bear
          but by summer we're already talking trash
          the season's changed but we don't see it coming
          he sits us down with the news
   a) she's going to come live with us and be your new
      mother
   b) you're going to have a new baby sister or brother
   c) we're moving to paris
          moving to paris, moving to paris…
the paris years: you will know them by my cries, short
      and sharp like knife wounds
too many to count but open them up and you'll tumble
      into my weltering world

beautifully hellish years, cute baby hell baby
in paris I learn a new language *you don't matter you're a*
defect you're a monster whom no one can love
    my birthday card says, you're ten years old not
zero one years old act your age and be a good girl
    problem child demon child devil child stupid
  girl ugly girl
movies on the champs-élysées
    galeries lafayette
        peaches at the marché
            un croissant et un pain au
  chocolat s'il vous plaît
            (I must learn to understand)
my trusty friend *la tour eiffel* watches over me as I walk
  alone to school
my heavy backpack no match for the speeding cars the
  gale force winds
    on the *métro* there are men
    their eyes their hands their half-moon faces
    their fingers their dancing eyebrows
    their naked scarlet dirty dicks right in my face
  my ten-year-old face my craning neck
    she just laughs when I tell her (is it *my* fault?)
chocolate cereal for breakfast football in *le parc*
    world cup blues
      les bleus
    my mind a hall of cracked mirrors
      I love paris
one day I take a bar of pink soap rub it all over the
  bathroom walls
but they don't read the writing

they just say don't do it again
but I do:
again
and again
and again
you should be as mature as a fifteen-year-old boy, they say
they say
so I take a pair of scissors open the closet door and cut
and cut
and cut
      I am the one
I am the one who cut her clothes to shreds
one friend tells her: just slap her, just slap her without
     warning
but still they don't see
(there's something wrong with the baby)
by then I've discovered a new thing
I watch it on the other families
in the hotels like cruise ships
by the pools
in the restaurants
why can't we be more like them?
but you're a disgrace you're disgusting you're a mistake you
     are dirty
you have no right to life
you're a terrible person
you're not even a person...
       he teaches me to love (but he doesn't know how
   to love)
       takes me into his lap in the dark and weeps
   (probably drunk at the time)

he says, she thinks it's just her baby just her baby
her baby
        (by now I am mute)
    we don't know anything, he says, we don't even
    know how to love
but I've found my escape hatch it's been there all along
    the slit in the membrane
the side door
I can slip in the wound
and it doesn't hurt here *and they can't find me here*
so I climb inside cast a spell remain a child forever
and they say, why don't you listen
they say, we just talked about this
they say, we've been talking about this for days
they say, where have you been
why are you never here
watch me in the paris years I'm slipping away I'm
    stuffing my mouth with cotton balls I'm growing
    scales on my body retractable spikes they can gouge
    into my skin and I won't feel a thing
just sew myself back up barbed wire black wiry thread
    dirty teddy bear
I can turn into a lizard turn into a reptile
I have slime in my veins for blood
I have learned a new language
        the world is not safe people are not safe
            but the thing is: *fish can't see water*

part one

in nairobi my sister tells me about the thunder. we lie
in our beds listening to the rain flogging the night outside.
from her top bunk she says, you just have to be careful
because it's when the thunder gets really loud that's when
it gets dangerous and people have to start packing out

from my lower bunk I listen for the rumble of thunder as
soon as I wake up but all I hear are the rumblings my
sister and I never talk about on the other side of the wall
like furniture being thrown down the stairs breaking
apart. I picture my mother flying tumbling legs feet over
head arms out grasping onto nothing like a newborn
baby falling… a sofa an empty fridge… broken doors…

      boom

            boom

                boom

                    down the stairs… busting

                      through the floor…

and I feel my own rumbling the wrench in my deepest
pit I always feel when I hear them fighting but my sister
does not stir from the top bunk so I do not stir

when my mother emerges from the rumbling room she acts like nothing's happened, her furnishings put right after the storm. she does not look into my eyes and I walk into the bathroom he's just come out of and there is urine all over the walls but I don't mention it to her, I don't mention it to anyone, instead I join my sister in the playroom and play like nothing's happened at dinner she sets the food on the table calm as a lull but she scolds me, why are you digging your fingers into your ears when you're about to eat and I think *why would you say that in front of him* and I wait for him to explode but he acts like he hasn't heard her

we sit on the living room floor, the tv box pitching its
rowdy lights, the two of them sit nearby in quiet talk so
I don't hear but all of a sudden he stands hurls his beer
and storms off, foam lathering her face, sliding down, she
squeezes her eyes shut bubbles licking her face holding it
all in, the froth, her breath, our shame

on the worst night the blood rushes from her nose, the rain sends its torrents but still he kicks us out and we stand damp before the gate of some ambassador's house. can you help us, she asks the guard, we have nowhere to go, and the guard says the master is sleeping but he lets us stay in the shed until morning. by the morning the rain has stopped, the blood has dried on her clothes in big brown flowers in lagos I sit at one end of my grandmother's large dining room table, at the other end my mother lifts a tumbler to her mouth and I watch the water disappear into her lips like a fish. she catches me in the courtyard, the front of my shirt all wrinkled up and soaked with my saliva and she asks, have you been chewing on your shirt?

no, I lie. *I fell in a puddle*

you're lying, she says, you've been chewing on your shirt.

no. I fell into a puddle

she grabs me by the arm. tell me the truth she says, her words florid with promise, you've been chewing on your shirt. my insides cave inwards but I stick with my story because I don't know what she'll do if I tell her the truth now. you're lying, you're lying, she says, her voice like black crayon scribbles, dragging me into my grandmother's house.

she lets us go stay with him for christmas because she doesn't know that we will not return.

at someone else's house we play hide-and-seek with the other kids. suddenly she's coming through the door her eyes on fire saying, this is ridiculous this is ridiculous they are my children, and he says, run and hide, and we do because he is the one who takes us to london and paris and restaurants and sports clubs and sends us to a school where the teachers don't beat us with canes and lives in a house where we have our own rooms so we don't have to sleep three to a bed.

we lock ourselves in the bathroom laughing like it's a game while she pounds on the door.

in paris we're allowed to spend one night with her at a
hotel. we sit on the bed the three of us watching a tv movie,
a true story about a woman who has to have her face
reconstructed after a car accident. when the woman on
tv unwraps the bandages from her head, touches her face
in wonder my sister and I are silent but my mother repeats
after the tv actress, giggling like a child: *je peux parler! je
peux parler.* and I think *I didn't know you knew any french*

she unpacks our takeout dinner on the hotel room
floor and she asks, have you started your period yet?

yes. her voice a ghost's whisper.

when did it start?

last december christmas.

and I think *I didn't know you started your period*

another year passes. she's reduced to cards and letters:

I do hope we'll see again, as your daddy promised, in january, when you have another holiday...

in london we're allowed to spend another night with her. she comes at us with her arms open wide saying, my babies, my babies. I freeze in her arms. she takes us to a high-rise building, a council flat with one bedroom and at night we get under the covers three to a bed again and she turns out the lights but I can't sleep, can't stop my desperate legs from seeking and she whispers fiercely in the dark, stay still! and I think *who are you to tell me to stay still?*

she is my mother. she tells me again and again as the years go by and I retreat further and further away from her: *I am your mother!*

but she doesn't know: I'd forgotten long ago what that meant.

everyone says I'm small for an eight-year-old. I'm tiny and skinny. at my new school I'm assigned to the dorm called teddy bears for the littlest girls and my sister is assigned to seals. I stand at the front of the classroom and the teacher asks me to introduce myself. it's halfway through the school year already. I say my name, how old I am. the kids snicker.

the showers are in another building, a dungeon leaking
slime, disinfectant razor-sharp on the walls, the floor.
I curl my toes because I'm afraid that mould will grow
between them. the water is never hot but we splash each
other anyway. we check each other's bodies for those
hairs springing between the legs, for chests rising like
dough. one girl stands under the corroded showerhead
making small circles on her forehead with her finger as
the trickle of water moistens her hair.

at bedtime we put our uniforms on hangers, our shoes beside our beds, we store our things in our lockers and matron comes to inspect. the day our father brought us for a tour they said teddy bears and I thought of bedtime stories in pyjamas but now I cry all the time and nobody knows why. some people say I'm homesick but even the youngest kids don't cry as much as me.

matron tells me to stop. she says, don't you know there are other kids here whose parents are really far away? don't you know there are kids here whose parents are dead? don't you see how you upset them when you cry? even my sister is sick of my crying. in the morning we stand at assembly under the sun's haze singing the national anthem. I find her among the rows of kids swaying in the heat. I start blubbering I'm homesick because that's what everyone says I am. my sister stares straight ahead, what am I supposed to do about it? no one knows, they just ask why do you cry all the time? one day someone says it's sensitive feelings, she has sensitive feelings. now my name is sensitive feelings girl and it feels good to have a name though they grow tired of me all the same. these sensitive feelings of yours, they say, they have to stop.

saturday mornings we congregate in the classrooms for
letter writing time. we write letters to our parents, our
blue-lined paper smudged pink with salt water and
matron grumbling at us for taking too long to bed down
for the night, our whispered battles and tattles after
lights out, matron coming back two three four how
many times in the night to tell us off and the time one of
the girls finds a lime-coloured snake in her bed and some
of the girls say it's bad luck to kill a snake, bad luck to
crush its head with your foot, we should toss it outside
into the bushes instead if only we can pluck up the
courage, but someone kills it and the girl cries and says
now she's going to die but she doesn't die. none of us do.

how about the movies we watch on saturday afternoons for movie time. huddled into the classroom with the shades drawn, the tv set is wheeled in on a cart. some movies we watch over and over again and we know all the lines, like *ratboy*. that one secretly scares us but we don't tell our parents that either.

what we most look forward to is friday night dinner of
roast chicken roast potatoes and ice cream for dessert. we
strategize to get the best piece of chicken because you're
only allowed one serving. when I get mine I pounce on it
about to dig in when I look up and see a girl staring at
her plate and I ask her what's wrong and she says, it's too
dry, it's just too dry, and I watch her eyes get plump, tears
splash onto her hand poking at the baked white flesh with
stainless steel and for once someone else is crying and
it's not me.

the next school term I graduate to the top bunk and I don't care that there are no railings on the bed until the night I find myself on the floor groping my way back up in the dark. the next morning the girls stare and ask what happened and my lower lip is split open, swollen and tingling with blood. but by now I have stopped crying.

I do other things instead. I run soft fabrics over my cheeks
and mouth and it's the only time I'm really quiet. I gnaw
at the cuffs of my sleeves. I squint in urgent morse code
and the kids make fun of me. but it's when I stop crying
that everyone starts to scream my name, in the classroom,
the dorms, at tennis practice, the teachers, matron and
the kids, my name a contagious flame-coloured bleat
stuck in their throats. the sound of my name, the sound
of what is wrong with you why do you behave like this
why are you so hyper? my name is hyper girl and one
night I punch a boy in the eye for no reason. he is smaller
than me and I'm summoned to see matron. before she says
anything I start to cry and she says, why are *you* crying?

at the end of the school year my report card flutters in
my father's hand declaring *behaviour problems* and
hyper-active and *annoying everyone around her.* he points
his finger at me and says, I don't want to see this kind of
thing on your report card ever again. then he goes to
paris to get our new apartment ready and find us a new
school. but still they scream my name, piercing holes
into me with their eyes. I don't do anything the way I'm
told. they say sit on the bed and watch the baby sleep in
her crib, make sure nothing happens while we make
dinner so I sit on the bed and watch the baby but there's
nothing else to do and they come back to find me asleep
on the bed and they are angry and they call him in paris
and he scolds me over the phone. what is wrong with me?

black mould has entered me creeping up like vines. when I speak I spew fungus and sulphur and the spores land on them. their real eyes peel off and they grow new eyes, eyes sealed over with fire and ice. they make me spend entire weekends in my room to make it stop. they make me kneel down and apologize for what I've done. they twist my ears until they burn but nothing works. by the time I'm ten years old I already know: I am a terrible person. my name is sensitive girl. hyper girl. *hated girl.*

backstage at the international school in paris the drama teacher wants me to put on some makeup but I'm not doing it right, I don't know what this brush is for what the blush is for. here, like this, she says and she takes the palette from me, takes the large brush with the soft bristles, just like how your mom does it, right? she looks at me, question marks popping all over her eyes. don't you ever watch your mom putting on makeup at home, she asks.

my mom?

our english teacher tells us to write about our families, arms us with maroon composition books and 2B pencils. *my older sister is twelve and in the seventh grade. I have a baby sister who is six months old. my father is a foreign correspondent...* this is the part where I'm supposed to write about my mother but I'm confused. which one do I say is my mother? the one that's here or the one I hardly remember? but I know these are questions I'm not supposed to ask. if I ask I'll get into trouble, might see that face that looks like someone is squirting lemon juice with pepper into his eyes, might hiss at me like a snake with sandpaper in its throat, and I remember what he told us: she's going to treat you like you're her own child.

my mother used to be an accountant. now she stays home to look after the baby.

there's a woman in our homeroom we've never seen before. she's not one of the teachers at school. our homeroom teacher says she's come to talk to us about changes. the woman takes each of us into a little room. sitting across from her, my hands clasped on my lap, our knees almost touching, she speaks in a voice soft as mist but I'm not sure what she's saying so I ask her to repeat it and she says it again. body odour, she says. there comes a time to start wearing deodorant, she says, when you get home let your mother know. so when I get home I tell her but she doesn't look up from what she's doing, just makes a small noise in the back of her throat and says, it's true, daddy said there was a time he was standing next to you and there was a very bad smell. it was so bad he couldn't stand it, she says in a high singing voice and she wrinkles her nose and scoots away from me like she's smelling it now.

our french teacher asks me a question but I don't have the answer, I don't even understand what she's asking me. she asks again and silence scuffs in, a billowing white mammoth taking up the empty chairs, but the teacher doesn't see it, she just wants an answer, doesn't see the big white hands swaddle me. she is screaming at me now: *mais c'est simple! infinitif! infinitif!* her face is a sandstorm, her voice of dried reeds thrashing in the wind. her hands are chopping the air. and I know that if we were anywhere else she would hit me. at the end of class when she's climbed down from her rage ship she turns to me as the students are filing out, cooling smoke rising from her eyes. you're lazy, she says.

in the courtyard of our apartment building one of their friends is scolding me. she has offered to take me and my sister out for the afternoon but she's finding that everyone is right about me. now she knows why whenever they see a child being spanked they turn to me and say, that's what you need. now she is yanking me by the arm. if you don't stop this behaviour I'm going to smack you, she says, and she looks like she's afraid. then my sister tells her, it's because she has mental problems, we took her to the doctors, but they couldn't figure out what was wrong with her. and she stops pulling on my arm and her eyes go round like clocks. later as we cruise down the champs-élysées my sister tells her it isn't true about the mental problems and the doctors, it was just a joke. oh my god, she says, and there are the little clocks again. I thought you were serious.

part two

in lagos she says maybe if we stand by the school gate every day at lunchtime daddy will drive by and see us and take us away from here. so we stand by the gate every day at lunch while the other kids screech and run in circles laughing in the school courtyard, and when he doesn't come and the bell rings we go back to our classrooms where we sit in rows and our uniforms are pink and grey and we wash them in the bathtub after school where they whip you across the back with a cane if you misbehave or don't listen or give the wrong answer and the cane feels like a burn across your back and we memorize the multiplication tables and the food burns and the dust burns and the air burns in your throat and there are green oozing gutters where I think alligators live and there is teargas and quicksand and open sores and it seems like just yesterday there was a garden of flowers with crêpe paper petals african violets and there were school plays and ballet and friends from belgium israel england america and trips to the snake park and the giraffe sanctuary, but now all I can do is jump in the neighbour's pool and pretend the shark from *jaws* is going to get me and I can scare myself watching *the day of the dead* with the other kids even though I know I'm not supposed to because I'm not old enough, I'm not even old enough to watch *thriller* but watching the big kids do all the moves helps me to forget to wish in paris she says why don't we write a letter to them and tape it to the door when we leave for school and they'll find it and they'll know how we feel. so we write them a letter, tape it to the door before we leave for school, say we don't want to live with you anymore, we want to go and live with mum, and even though we haven't seen her in more than two years and I don't remember her I agree because it must be better than this

and we come home from school and they've found the letter and they are angry and tell us how dare you say you're unhappy after everything we do for you, and it's your fault if you're unhappy (it's your fault nobody showed up to your birthday party, it's your fault your bike was stolen, it's your fault you don't speak your father's tongue your mother's tongue, it's your fault you're not close to your aunts and uncles, it's your fault your little sister is misbehaving because you make her think that every time is playing time, it's all your fault the ornament broke because you didn't bring me a napkin) and how could you write that letter, she says to me again later sidling up next to me at the sink where I'm washing the dinner dishes, don't you know you broke your father's heart

and I begin to build a world of my own harvesting rubies and gemstones from the movies tv shows other families build an ark I can climb into night after night learn to weave an invisible cape to cloak myself in by day and I know it's wrong so I don't tell anyone not even my sister even though we used to build worlds together but I know this is different because I'm stealing what I don't deserve to have in limassol after he rages at us in his hotel room and tells us he hates us so much and we slink back to our hotel room like tiny criminals, she says do you think if we wished hard enough just wished really hard we'd be away from here, we'd be with mum, and I'm surprised she's saying this because she's more than old enough to know that of course we won't, and I don't want to be with mum anyway, I know exactly where I want to be and no plane or train or boat can take me there, and I'm already away from here so that on road trips when we're stuck in the back of the car while they fight in the front and it's torture (you're too cantankerous! you started it!) I can escape until I hear him scream my name and I come back to find that he's banging his hands on the steering wheel and shouting, I send you to a good school and you never have anything to say!

in abidjan we have a house with a pool two cats two dogs a maid a gardener and parties for the expat friends but there are no pictures of us on the walls or on the dining room buffet and daddy's cereal goes here and your cereal goes there and don't use this towel use the old towels you always get the towels dirty last time they were all black and we must soak the fruit from the market in bleach solution before we eat it and we don't eat lunch in this house and if I see even a drop of water on the dishes I'll scream and you can't fold the napkins like that, that's anarchy and you cut mango like a little child don't you, you're such a disappointment and you can't use my cup, if you were nice girls who cleaned things properly I would let you use my cup and get out of my bathroom you won't clean it properly, if you would clean it properly you could use my bathroom, but you must never say you don't want to come home because we pay your school fees, and that's how you learn that some prisons have invisible iron bars, but I don't need to say it anyway because I've learned how to be here and not be here, so I say nothing at the dinner table even when he regales us with tales about the time he was reporting from a hotel rooftop in liberia and the hotel was bombed and they all had to escape because I know it's the penalty I have to pay so I have to get up and greet him when he comes home like I'm happy to see him even though I dread them coming home and I hate every moment and have always hated hated hated every moment and I only want to get away and only when they leave the house and I'm alone do I turn into myself turn the music up and even though he likes to say you're not at war with anybody in this family, he doesn't realize that he is the war they are the war and we are all the war

a monster child
watching the world
from the crevice in the
crawlspace every once in
a while I put on a human
suit go out and collect
stories scraps of humanity
shreds of life mementos
from the human world
I collect a big silver grin
hidden beneath my painted
mesh to take back
to my cell and weave

you get too close I
have scales and rough
skin I have a thousand
eyes that never close at
night I go down long
tunnels long corridors
I take my lantern and
crawl into a hole in
the dark I stay
there all night
millennia pass but
there is no time
here I want to stay

into a dream of someday
it will be human like
them and they'll never know
they don't know they think
they know they think I'm
just like them they are
looking for me they come to
my house but I'm in a dungeon
in a cellar bound and gagged
and shackled to the wall the
person who came to answer
the door is a hologram I
grow spikes no one sees
no one can see spikes on the
inside where near me and it
turns wonderous who

here forever not
back up there with
them where it feels
like wearing a
coat made out of
darkenened
cities.

49

part three

a guest comes to the house, sits with her in the living room talking. I stand in the doorway waiting for her to introduce me. her eyes flick towards me, two tiny storms in a forest. she blinks once, twice, turns her eyes back to the guest. finally I introduce myself, my words tumbling to the ground like nestling birds, all fluffy pinfeathers and wisps. and she sits with her arms crossed, blinking cottony light from her eyes, saying nothing, saying everything.

on new year's eve I hide in the hotel bathroom just as the fireworks are starting and he says where is she tell her to get out here and someone says she doesn't want to and he says what do you mean she doesn't want to and he barges through the door and says with bullets in his voice you have to get out here and I cry but I get out there and when he comes home from work he says where is she and they say she's in her room and he says she's always in her damn room and they make me come out of my room but they never ask why I'm always in my damn room so I talk to them on the phone from school every weekend because I have to even though it feels like a swarm of bees in my throat a stomachfull of wasp stings my anger a pile of diamonds lining my stomach and when my little sister begs me to sleep in the bed with her in the hotel I say no even though the bed is more than big enough for both of us because I have tiny spikes sticking out all over my body can't you see

when their mothers come to visit the girls rocket out of
the dorms and cross the courtyard their breath jangling
don't stop runnin' till you reach your mother's arms and
when it's my turn they say your mum's here and I say okay
and they say run and I say okay and they say run run and
they see the way I'm moving and they shriek you act like
you don't *love* your mother and it feels like a red ant spraying
formic acid in my face and there's no suitcase big enough
to stuff the silence that follows me across the courtyard
hope they don't see it falling out my pockets out my
clenched fists don't you know shame echoes shame bleeds
hope they can't see me, my legs moving through the
burning syrup, the mountains watching in a ring around
the courtyard shoulders crusted in thick white capes

I want to be like the girls at school chiming in when the ads come on, my mum uses beef stock! my mum uses powder cleaner! my mum uses vinegar! and I listen in awe but I have nothing to add because I know I am not like them and when the news comes on the red news the blue news the how-could-anyone-do-that news crushing their glowing bodies squeezing them till they make salt diamonds in the corners of their eyes while I make small sounds in my throat so they don't notice my wordless hole the bluegrey smoke where my mouth should be they don't notice my famished maw fill with blood tapeworms chopped-up a thousand ripped-off lips writhing wriggling slithering drunk with the deeds of the boys with their guns with their pimples with their mugshots my tiny music box playing machine guns needle bombs missiles blades steak knives shredded flesh flying hair innards organs entrails playing over and over and over and over again grinding stones in my gut but how do you tell and I know from the way they say mum and dad they mean it and no matter what they say they will all go back to their parents in the end leaving me alone

part four

l was not conceived
l am a creature formed beneath
your damp floorboards, an alien
dumped and forgotten on earth
l have no mother no father
   no pre-history no antecedents
l am nobody's baby sister
              or big sister
l am nobody's baby nobody's daughter
l have never been a girl or a boy
l have no connection to anything
l am an abortion beneath the earth
l am not human l cannot reproduce
or replicate, l ask nothing of my
   parents and l require nothing
   l don't even know what they're for
   l am a broken bird
      caught in an oil slick
   trapped
      underneath scaffolding

who taught you how to love don't you know nothing grows on desert planets don't you know that shipwrecked thing stuck inside you that grill tarsticky with dead birds' wings lungs won't work don't you know that twisted up speckled thing used to be an organ that thing clogged with dead leaves deadbaby bones burned flesh oil spill musk tar grease and bat guano ever since I was a little girl I have been a guttersnipe reaching for the queen's silky lace but who do you think you are this is not for people like you please do not soil it with your dirty hands

I want to speak the language you speak of I loved him
    so deep and I miss him so much
words like *memorial service* and *I'm sorry for your loss* like
    t-shirts and bubble gum rich travellers bring
to the kids in the slums
               more than anything in the world
slides from your safaris your lions giraffes your rhinos hyenas
who ever knew such a thing existed as you

but I can steal it and they'll never know no one will ever know, they just say I can't believe you didn't shed a tear on the last day of school you have no feelings they say but they don't know how I stay close to the ground, sweep the ocean floor for I know there's black gold trapped underneath. and don't you know at home we have this book called *baby & child* and when the baby gets sick and everyone cries and holds her and rocks her and I just stand in the middle of the room blinking and they say she's a hard one she has no sympathy for anybody, they don't know how I pore over that book, lick the pages like that famished child licking up the grease on a discarded newspaper that once held fish and chips, don't you know what is glistening on those pages like sugar sprinkled on doughnuts. so I watch them run into their fathers' arms, watch them claw goodbye at the train station tears studding their faces like jewels and while they say if my mum died I'd be suicidal I'd never be the same again I couldn't cope I really couldn't cope, I collect their heartbreaks their heart attacks their car crashes their cancers their funeral processions and at night under my covers I bring it out turn it over in my hands big and pink and rough as a hunk of rose quartz its dry brittle branches tickling my throat that piranha feeding on my soft insides that demon crack-addicted black-tailed jackrabbit comes to chomp me to bits at night and I sniff around gravestones in cemeteries like a bloodhound and I scour the sites of their tragedies their catastrophes their disasters the way a vulture scavenges the remains for what they dropped before the tv cameras and the microphones for what is sticking to the rubble I scrape it off take it home string it together on my invisible mobile hanging above my bed and I never sleep

part five

she is happy but I don't know why. it's in the tango of her hands, the clip of her steps, the flash of her teeth when she says, what do you like to eat, what do you girls like for breakfast? she takes us food shopping filling a basket with the things that are supposed to make us happy— yoghurt, custard, baked beans, white bread, jam, cereal, milk. finally after three years she can decorate her flat. from behind my oozing scrim, silent and dismembered, I watch her.

I am an animal I am a lizard

she says who is your best friend and I give her a name any name. she says what's your favourite subject at school and I just shrug. I'm her talking doll gone silent. the one you got for your birthday that blinks when you put her on her back cries when you shake her and talks when you squeeze her hand. you've spent hours playing with her and then one day you come back from a long trip and pull her out of the toy box and find that she's gone silent. you shake her and her eyes roll crazily in her head and you squeeze her hand like you used to but she just stares back at you her eyes vacant.

you were such a happy baby

maybe she's remembering the child who left her more than three years ago.

but I don't seem to remember anything. she asks me, don't you remember this auntie? don't you remember this uncle? don't you remember your cousin so-and-so? I shake my head. she says it seems like everybody remembers you but you don't remember anybody. and I have nothing to offer in reply just my glassy silence. and I see something new sneak into her eyes. she looks at me as if I have scars all over my body.

it was just three years...

even though I don't remember anyone she wants me to talk to them on the phone. she clings to the phone like it's a life raft. she says we have call waiting now so when someone calls while you're on the phone you'll hear a beep and you can just click over. I say okay, but I don't care. the call waiting doesn't excite me or impress me. there are things I want to say, things that make ripping noises rupture flesh and draw blood. things like barbed wire coiled up inside me unspooling. when she finds out that I hear the beep but I don't click over her face crumples up: sometimes I find your attitude so disgusting!

but I know already. *I am a bad child I am a monster*

my mouth is stitched up with coarse thread. the spikes growing out of me are the size of an infant's limbs. she can't see them but she can feel them. one day she asks if she can have a hug because she needs one. I retract my spikes just long enough to let her approach. her arms encircle me and I'm as frozen as a prey animal under attack. she never tries it again. but it's not like she hugs my sister either. no one can move in the thickness of my silence. it is contagious. she gets a bigger tv. she stares at the box as if it's going to save us. she studies the tv guide. we eat silent dinners in front of the blinking lights. sometimes she has the money to take us to buy new jeans or to see a musical and when I pretend to sleep through the performance she says you don't know how to be happy, you didn't even laugh.

monster child

she says you never want to bring any friends home
because you don't think this house is good enough, do
you. that's not why I never bring any friends home, but I
don't say anything. from my distant station where I
observe human life I watch her happiness fade like lights
flickering off across a cityscape. she puts on weight, she
moves more slowly. I have cut her up and sewn her back
together time and time again. she says I seem cold and
unloving. but I know. I am an impostor. I have my own
language my own culture. I have to keep the truth inside
until it's safe to come out. so when she tells me she wishes
I would show emotion I say nothing but in my mind I
see the baseball bat I would need to smash her entire
living room to pieces. the tv the stereo the little white
vases with the polyester flowers.

how about that for fucking emotion

a thousand and one nights we spend in front of the
television set. game shows, talk shows, american sitcoms.
from her favourite spot on the sofa she launches her
missiles softly.
she says, I'm tired of you treating me like this.
she says, the day I will understand this daughter of
    mine...
she asks, why are you so damn impossible?
she looks to me for all the answers.
but a small animal can be clubbed to death and never
    make a sound.

my family see me as a bad
person and that I'm the cause
of all the badness in me.
But it's not all my fault that
they see me as bad or ~~or~~ not
loving them. Because of the way
they treated me I have lost
connection with people and I
feel dirty and worthless. I feel like
I'm already d[e]ad and I'm no
longer human.
because I was
a wonderful p[erson]
affectionate who
fullest And ~~they~~ I
a way ~~want to~~
want to be a[t]
person that I
I want my fa[mily]
I'm bad. I want
thinking I'm bad
hard, and st[ay]
n my own

so terrible.
who I lost conse[nse]
stopped breathing
be resustated
would have on a dirty
                floor

But my honour
big secret n[o] e[a]
ships and guilty
being tired - I feel like a[ll]
all this stupid fault.

_____ for:

can't go to someone
___ say, "I need help"
because I wouldn't

In my head I don't seem to be able to tell them
have any parents ___ what ~~who~~ wrong and
would feel so
terrible.

I'm never going to
be normal; I'm never
going to be able to be
happy because I'm
already dead. I am
at ~~her~~, I can't
even talk to anyone
about myself because
I feel so terrible.
something wrong,
feel like the most
evil thing in the
world. I want to
be able to be pure
like I was meant
to be

People look at me and
think I'm so happy
and life is so hopeful
for me — but they
don't know the truth
I think I could ~~kill~~
myself sometimes
can't take it. I
feel like I have done
any can comfort me.
I have no means of escape;
I can't talk to anyone...
there isn't even anywhere
to go to be alone

I can't stand everyday
life.
I can't bear to face
another day.
Sometimes it gets to a
point where I don't look
- I can take it anymore.
Sometimes I come close
to running away.
Sometimes I think I should
kill myself. But then But then But then
I just can't bear to go on
& there and see people

in my second boarding school I make a promise to myself after lights out, the other girls asleep, blanket pulled over my head, I vow into the dark: *by the time I'm thirteen, I want to be fixed.*

there are children on the sides of buses, on waiting room posters, on tv spots, my brothers and sisters, their heads tucked into their elbows, legs drawn into triangles, clutching broken-necked teddies leached of colour, clothes greased from donation bins. and the radio spots say, *help protect a child this christmas,* they say, *this christmas all she wants is to not get punched anymore,* and every time I see those children I feel a cramp stitch along my sides but it's not from a punch because all my bruises are on the inside so no one can see them and I wish I could be one of those children on the sides of the buses so maybe the charity that makes those radio spots could see me too.

when the girls at school cry they let the tears sop their
faces and they let you put your arms around them and
when I cry I cover my face with my hands and they say why
do you hide when you cry why are you ashamed to cry?

on a visit home from school my mother takes me by surprise one day. she doesn't look up from the tv, doesn't stop chewing her dinner when she says, maybe we should send you to a psychologist, and I say nothing but a door opens inside me and my heart does a pirouette in the light that spills in because I've seen those talk shows where the psychologist comes out and sits next to the school bully and says, I look at her and I see a hurting child. but then the days pass and the weeks pass and nothing happens and I remember the time she said, distress prickling her voice, we should go and take some family photos every other family has family photos why don't we have family photos, and my sister and I nodded solemnly, staring at the television set, but that was the last we heard of it and we never did go and get the family photos.

I know the helpline number by heart. I've had it scribbled down on a scrap of paper and I've walked around with it in my wallet for months like it's a lucky charm but there's no way I can call from home because my mother will find out. so I call from a payphone and someone picks up and says, hello you're through to childline, and I can't tell if the voice is male or female and I can't get any words out, I can only breathe into the phone, and the voice waits a beat or two and then they say, would you *like* to speak? but they sound like the teachers at school when they're cross with you. I hang up.

one day when I'm home alone a pair of jehovah's witnesses pay a visit to the house. it's a mother and her son, a boy around my age. the mother says, can I talk to you, what's your name, and I give her a fake name and I let her speak but only because I'm curious about the boy who stands silently behind her while she does all the talking. but I'm not listening, I can't keep my eyes off the boy, staring at me, his face stiff as a wax mask, his eyes communicating nothing. but I can almost hear the tears splashing on tile, I can see it in his eyes: he looks like he wants to die.

I call the helpline again. this time a man picks up and this time I beat back the silence before it claps its hands over my mouth. when I'm finished the man speaks with the hush of a priest but his voice tells me he's talked to a hundred kids that day, that he can't wait for his shift to be over so he can commute home on the bus sit in front of the telly… he concludes with, I know it's 'ard but give 'er a hug, tell 'er you don't wanna go to boardin' school no more. on the walk home I turn it over in my mind: *he didn't understand a single word I said.*

in a doctor's office I find a leaflet for a woman who has
me meet with her on saturday afternoons. her voice is
warm and amber like a radio host's but that's all. one day
she calls the house while I'm out and when I come home
my mother sings out from the bathroom saying someone
called and said she can't meet with you this saturday but
she'll see you next week.

oh no. she's just a friend, I say.

she sounds so mature, my mother says and it's a
good thing she can't see my face.

the jehovah's witnesses come back. I pass them on the street as I'm leaving the house one day. I try to sneak by but the boy sees me and we lock eyes and before the wax can start to melt he gives me away, murmuring to his mother, mum, mum, isn't that her? and she scrutinizes my face and says my name but it's not my real name anyway so I say, I'm sorry you've got the wrong person, and I walk on. the boy says nothing.

in my third boarding school I keep having headaches and I can't sleep so they send me to the school nurse. at first she tries massaging my scalp but it doesn't help so we sit in her office and I tell her some of my stories. she says, I used to cry a lot when I was your age, and she stares at me like she's waiting for the tears to start and I know it's my cue but all I can do is stare back. she says, you're desperate to be loved, aren't you, just desperate to be loved. and all I can do is look away.

so you still won't tell me your deep dark secret but that's okay, she says, and she scribbles down a name and address on a pad of paper and she sends me to see another woman outside the school because she's only a nurse after all and there are other kids to tend to and the new woman has a quiet office and a sofa and a wall of books and a box of tissues and I like the way she listens, her smooth manicured hands that remind me of birds and the way she says, finally: some people can be really stupid when it comes to children.

thank you

*to all whose support, guidance and generosity
helped in the creation of this book*

margo zysman
lindsay r. allison
david moratto
david james brock
sophia apostol and firefly creative writing
ira yakobson
lana lehr
kathy friedman and inkwell workshops
bieke stengos
hanan hazime
adria vasil
sabrina ward harrison and megan love
marlee liss
mohamed abdulkarim ali
the writers' union of canada
league of canadian poets

further resources

articles
◆◆◆

Parlee, Jennifer, et al. "The Fragmented Child: Disorganized Attachment and Dissociation." York University. The Trauma & Mental Health Report: Sharing Knowledge on Trauma & Mental Health with the Community, 2013. http://trauma. blog.yorku.ca/2013/04/the-fragmented-child-disorganized-attachment-and-dissociation/.

Spinazzola, Joseph, et al. "Childhood Psychological Abuse as Harmful as Sexual or Physical Abuse." American Psychological Association, 2014. https://www.apa.org/news/press/releases/2014/10/psychological-abuse.

books
◆◆◆

Biever, John A. and Maryann Karinch. *The Wandering Mind: Understanding Dissociation from Daydreams to Disorders.* Plymouth: Rowman & Littlefield Publishers, Inc., 2012.

Bradshaw, John. *Healing the Shame That Binds You.* Deerfield Beach: Health Communications, Inc., Expanded and updated ed., 2005.

Courtois, Christine A. *It's Not You, It's What Happened to You: Complex Trauma and Treatment.* Dublin: Telemachus Press, 2020.

Courtois, Christine A. and Julian D. Ford. *Treatment of Complex Trauma: A Sequenced, Relationship-Based Approach.* New York: The Guilford Press, 2016.

Walker, Pete. *Complex PTSD: From Surviving to Thriving: A Guide and Map for Recovering from Childhood Trauma.* Azure Coyote Publishing, 2013.

resources
◇◇◇

ACEs Connection: https://www.acesconnection.com/.

Beacon House: https://beaconhouse.org.uk/.

Center on the Developing Child: Harvard University: https://developingchild.harvard.edu/science/key-concepts/toxic-stress/.